C000184197

THROUGH RAISING YOUR GAME

67

KICK-ARSE

Philosophies

FOR SMALL BUSINESS OWNERS

GEORGE SWIFT

Published by Bigger Brighter Bolder Publishing Ltd. 144 Broadway, Didcot, OX11 8RJ.

ISBN: 978-1-9993333-0-0
Cover design by Anne-Marie Lockett,
Phase Two Design.
Printed in the UK.

CONTENTS

DEDICATION

This book is dedicated to Tracey Miller, my partner in life and in business. Together we have created something truly special with Bigger Brighter Bolder, BBB Success Groups and Extreme Growth Masterminds. As I always say, if it wasn't for her, I'd be teaching great shit to empty rooms.

Tracey's continued confidence and support have given me the time and space to develop my ideas and philosophies, as well as a platform and audience to share them with. I simply wouldn't be in this position without her. I'm constantly reminded by our members and clients that, "Every business needs a Tracey."

WELCOME

Welcome to 67 KICK-ARSE Philosophies for Small Business Owners. To get the most out of this content, please download the free accompanying workbook that gives you a clear process to help you identify your own gaps in your game. To download, visit:

www.BiggerBrighterBolder.co.uk/67Workbook

As an ambitious small business owner, I would love to welcome you to my free Facebook community where I regularly share ideas, content and Q&As:

www.facebook.com/groups/BiggerBrighterBolder

Let's begin ...

INTRODUCTION

Just like every great story, the story of your life has a lead character. You.

Every lead character who has ever gone on a quest has had to walk two paths. They've had to navigate the external world, with all its challenges, antagonists and conquests. They've also had to navigate their own internal landscape, conquering their demons, doubts and fears. They've had to grow as people to overcome the challenges that could have thwarted their progress in the external world.

The two paths intertwine with one another. Progressing on the outward journey will force you to overcome internal obstacles, while clearing away internal obstacles will enable you to handle the external challenges.

The hero's quest is one that always follows these two paths. Your story will similarly unfold.

This book is the amalgamation of some of my core personal development and business growth philosophies from my BBB Success Groups and Extreme Growth Masterminds. It's intended as a call to action, to encourage you, a small business entrepreneur, to raise your game and step up to be the business owner your business needs you to be, so that you can achieve your full potential.

This book is for the business owner who wants to bridge the gap between who they are today and who they need to become, so they can bridge the gap between the business they operate now and the business they want to run.

Broken down into easy to digest sections, this book can be read cover to cover or dipped into as a regular source of inspiration. My work is dedicated to helping business owners who are willing to help themselves. The business owners who are tenacious, persistent and prepared to fight, and the underdogs who are driven to create something of purpose and who dare to dream. If you identify with any of that, this book is written for you!

ON PERSONAL DEVELOPMENT

Small businesses don't fail, their owners do.

As a small business owner, your business will survive, thrive or die based on your efforts alone. You don't get to blame external factors such as recession or other climate changes. These don't affect your ability to grow even though a huge company may struggle to survive. You're more nimble, can evolve, react and adapt where necessary. You're agile.

If you want your business to grow, you must grow. Your business is an extension of you. It reflects and magnifies who you are at its core. Your values and your strengths will be present, as will your fears and limitations. You are your business's greatest asset, and its biggest liability. When you're on top form, your business benefits. When you struggle, your business struggles. If you reach your personal limit and plateau, your business will plateau.

At BBB, our motto is, "Your business is your business. You're our business." In other words, we exist to help you, the owner, become who you need to be. We support and help you create and grow the business you want. For this reason, I don't position myself as a business coach. I work on you, so you can work on your business. The vast number of success stories coming out of my Success Groups and Extreme Growth Masterminds are testimony to the effectiveness of my philosophy. Your business needs you to step up and be all you can be, so it can be all it can be.

To check out Success Groups, go to:
www.BiggerBrighterBolder.co.uk

Success is a journey of 2 paths. The inner path and the outer path. You must walk them both.

Just like every great story, the story of your life has a lead character. You.

Every lead character who has ever gone on a quest has had to walk two paths. They've had to navigate the external world, with all its challenges, antagonists and conquests. They've also had to navigate their own internal landscape, conquering their demons, doubts and fears. They've had to grow as people to overcome the challenges that could have thwarted their progress in the external world.

The two paths intertwine with one another. Progressing on the outward journey will force you to overcome internal obstacles, while clearing away internal obstacles will enable you to handle the external challenges.

Think of any film or book you enjoy and you'll see that, regardless of whether it's a romantic comedy, tragedy or action film, the hero's quest is one that always follows these two paths. Your story will similarly unfold.

Mastering life is a combination of working on the internal and external environments. In business terms, this is working on any internal limitation or block that prevents you from growing your business and successfully navigating the business terrain.

First, we are a product of our environment. Then our environment is a product of us.

You've no doubt heard the notion that we are all a product of our environment. Normally this is used within the context of violent criminals, or to explain undesirable characteristics. But it's also true of wealthy, successful and healthy people, and those with happy, long-lasting relationships. We are all products of our environment.

For instance, if we were born into starvation and violence, we'd be a very different person than if we'd been born into abundance and peace. Studies show that a mother's experience of her 'world' directly impacts the brain development of her unborn baby. The unborn child is already adapting to the environment awaiting it. Throughout our lives, our environment continues to shape us, but none more so than in our early years.

You may or may not like doing it, but take a look at your past as within it sits the clues to your blocks and barriers, fears and doubts, expectations and standards. Left unchecked, we naturally perpetuate the environment we grew up in.

If you're not happy with the idea of your past equalling or defining your present and future, you need to get fully engaged in changing the course of your life. If you don't, history has a canny knack of repeating itself. The good news is, change is completely possible.

If you're going to push life to the limits, you'd better know how the engine works!

If you only use your car to pop to the shops and back, you don't need to know how it works. If something goes wrong, you pick up the phone and someone with a van comes to sort it out. However, if you wanted to go on a round-the-world adventure, you'd definitely want to have mechanical knowledge.

As an entrepreneur, it's the same with your brain, specifically knowing how to get the most out of it. Should you hit a tricky patch, you need to know how to overcome the challenges, push yourself further and stay motivated. You may well hit the limits of your performance and there's no man in a van you can call to fix things. You can get support and guidance, but no-one can do it for you. Only you can metaphorically pop your bonnet and make the necessary repairs.

My philosophy is to educate, to shine a light on issues, blocks and barriers, offer up a mirror with which to honestly see yourself, and offer you new perspectives through which to view yourself and your life. I'll help you learn for yourself, so you can apply what's needed to get the most out of your own adventure, going beyond what you may have thought possible.

Who's the boss?

95%-99% of everything you think feel and do is unconscious. Your unconscious brain is forty times faster and a million times more powerful than you (your conscious brain). Your unconscious runs the show. It's the boss.

If you leave it to its own devices, your unconscious brain will drive your life along a predetermined path based on your learnings and experiences to date, that will almost certainly limit you from achieving your potential.

It does this through stimulating biological and chemical impulses to manipulate actions, reactions, behaviours and therefore results. You are on autopilot and unless you start to learn how to take the controls, you'll keep getting the same results.

Your unconscious brain is big, fast and powerful, like a charging elephant. How do you take control of that? You can't outrun it or wrestle it. You must use the only advantage you have. Your unconscious brain isn't smart. It has the intelligence of a 5-year old. You need to learn how to outwit it with your far smarter conscious brain. You need to become the boss. It is possible.

Most people do what feels better to them, over what is better for them. Don't let your emotions bullshit you out of your success.

You can't trust your feelings. Some people will say the opposite, that your feelings are road signs to some inner wisdom. And while I do think there's an inherent wisdom that sometimes comes into play, our feelings are the result of chemistry triggered by our brain's biological impulses. These impulses are reactions to data being fed into the unconscious brain through the senses, that are cross-referenced against the stored data of our experiences and learnings. Feelings are what the unconscious brain uses to manipulate actions in any given set of circumstances.

The entire animal kingdom has similar internal processes and biological systems to ours, but they lack the awareness of them. It's our awareness of these manipulating forces that we call emotions and feelings. They're the by-product of chemicals rushing through our bodies, stimulating actions and behaviours.

You can't trust your feelings because you can't fully trust the creator of those feelings – your unconscious brain. If feelings are road signs, they're those laid out by a child. Remember, the unconscious brain isn't smart. Trusting your feelings is like trusting a toddler with the keys to your car and expecting them to drive you safely to work. Feelings of fear will hold you back. Doubt will slow you down. Lust could get you in a whole heap of trouble. Boredom can lead you down a wrong path. Sometimes, you have to ignore your feelings and trust your conscious brain (you), to know what's right for you.

Dominate your success by eliminating the gaps in your game.

It can be scary to look honestly and authentically at yourself. When you do, you'll see gaps. Gaps between who you are now and who you need to be to achieve what you want to achieve. Gaps between what you have and what you'd like to have. Between your health now and the health you'd like in the future. Between the relationship you're in versus the one you'd like to be in. Between the business success you want and what you have now.

But it's in these gaps that you'll find the secrets to why you're not achieving what you want to achieve.

Your gaps could include skills, knowledge, resources, systems and processes. But of most interest here are the gaps in you: your mindset, attitude and behaviours that are stopping you from achieving what you want and can achieve. You may have confidence gaps, self-esteem or worthiness gaps. You might lack passion, drive and motivation, or not have a clear vision. You may need an aspiration boost. You might be plagued by doubts or fears.

Once you get used to the process of looking for and into the gaps, it stops being scary and starts to feel exhilarating. A gap for me represents an opportunity to grow, to advance and to enhance life. I dare you to look at your gaps.

Success and happiness start with self-esteem.

Sounds fluffy I know, but your self-esteem limits what you can achieve by setting the bar low for what you feel you deserve. If you start to become more successful than you think you deserve to be, you'll start to feel uncomfortable. Unconscious mechanisms will manipulate you 'back to where you belong'. Equally, your overall happiness and wellbeing are directly linked to your self-esteem.

This is why it's important to invest time in boosting your self-esteem and general sense of self. Here are just some of the ways you can positively impact your self-esteem:

1. Limit contact with people who knock you, bring you down or doubt your ability. Instead spend time with people who make you feel good about yourself.
2. Limit exposure to those environments that don't support you in who you want to be – find your tribe, other people who understand the journey you're on and what it is to be an entrepreneur.
3. Monitor your self-talk and don't allow negative thoughts about yourself to go unchecked. Instead, make a conscious effort to initiate positive self-talk.
4. Keep a diary or journal and track your achievements each day, every day, no excuses.

A healthy self-esteem will raise the bar for what you deserve, and therefore what you can achieve. It will also massively and positively impact your overall experience and quality of life.

ON BUSINESS

That "Work 'ON' your business not 'IN' your business" bullshit!

You've heard it over and over again, and it's become accepted as conventional business wisdom, but that won't stop me calling "Bullshit!" on it.

Of course you need to be working 'ON' your business, I don't have a problem with that. The problem I have is the not 'IN' your business part of this throw-away statement.

It might be the aim of bigger business owners to eventually exit the business, but for most small business owners, if you're not working 'IN' your business, you're not making money. This is why it's such a dangerous universal meme. Initially, you will most likely want to be 'IN' your business as much as possible, because that's when you're earning. Grow your business, achieve some financial success, then you can outsource, hire and start increasing your 'ON' business work.

The statement implies that working 'IN' your business is somehow not as important as 'ON' your business. This can trick smaller business owners into thinking they're working hard when they're sitting around thinking shit up, devising marketing strategies or generally fucking about on non-income-generating tasks.

It's a perfect example of business bullshit that gets bandied about as conventional wisdom, but which can seriously hinder or misdirect a small business owner.

The smart entrepreneur knows when to do more and when to do different.

Contrary to the popular wisdom that says you should work smarter, not harder, we know anecdotally, and from the autobiographies of successful people, that you HAVE to work hard if you want to achieve anything of real substance. Many small business owners simply aren't working hard enough, and part of the problem is the "work smart not hard" bullshit they've been sold.

Being successful is about working hard AND being smart enough to know when hustling harder, grinding more or working your arse off isn't the right solution. In some situations, just doing more isn't going to solve anything and can even make the problem worse. In these instances, the smart entrepreneur knows to be creative, to come up with clever solutions to problems and not just work more, faster, harder.

To be a smart, successful entrepreneur, the skill is knowing when to work harder and do more, and when to work smarter and be more creative.

Once your mindset and attitude are in place, the gap is in your business model.

If I wasn't in the personal performance, mindset, attitude and behaviour arena, I'd definitely be in the business modelling game. The right mindset and attitude are key ingredients for success. However, while the greatest mindset will ring the last drop of potential out of the weakest business model, it can't perform miracles. A great mindset and approach need a great business model to deliver great results. Get these two elements in place, and you and your business will be rocking.

The business model I share contains 7 cogs. If you get the right cogs in place, your business model will generate money. You then need to consistently turn the handle. The 7 cogs are:

Do the right thing

Do it the right way

Find the right customer

Set the right price

Create the right sales strategy

Work with the right people (employees, partners etc)

Implement the right systems and processes

Any weakness in any of these cogs will reduce the productivity of the model. Getting it right can take time; you'll need to implement, take feedback, learn, innovate, implement and repeat. But spend time making robust cogs and you'll have a robust, profitable business.

Make sure you're in the right gear for the right conditions.

Most business advice is generic. As your business grows, your needs and those of your business will evolve and change. Be wary of cookie-cutter approaches and strategies, they may not be suitable for where you're at and could even be harmful to your business growth.

Selecting the right strategy for your business is much like selecting the right gear when driving. You want the gear that's appropriate for the current conditions. Much of what's being taught for business would bury a start-up struggling to get going. A start-up business applying a £1M strategy is equivalent to a car trying to pull away in top gear.

As your business grows, it needs to effectively transition through the gears and upgrade its strategies. A 6-figure business applying a start-up or 5-figure strategy would be like a car trying to join a motorway in first gear. Smooth business growth is equivalent to seamlessly working your way up through the gears. You want to use the full range of gears, while not continually bouncing off the rev limiter.

If you're not into car analogies, this simply translates as needing a strategy that takes you to the next evolutionary stage of your business, transitioning before your model runs out of room for growth.

Outsource ASAP

It's important to free yourself to work on the specific areas of your business that you're best placed to deliver, and which return the greatest financial rewards for effort and time.

Don't try to do everything on your own. I know it sounds and feels bloody heroic to singlehandedly circumnavigate the globe, climb Everest, sail the oceans or grow your business, but it often ends in disaster. Business is a team sport, and you want to start getting your winning team in place as soon as possible.

Businesses with high levels of funding apply a very different growth strategy to your average small business. They put the team, structure, systems and processes, technology and infrastructure in place, then grow into them.

Small businesses typically have to grow organically, which can be slow and laborious. Make life easier on yourself by outsourcing intelligently. Initially outsource your low return/low cost jobs, to allow yourself to put your efforts into high yield tasks. This includes getting a cleaner, gardener or housekeeper for home chores. Put the time you save into the greatest revenue-generating tasks, typically sales activities. As you grow, hire more expensive talent to plug the gaps in your game.

Success is like the leaves on a tree. The causes of your success are the branches and trunk. Feed the roots and the tree will take care of itself.

When you focus on the results of your success, and not the causes, you can nurture the wrong aspects of your business. Equally, if the 'tree' that is your business is bearing no fruit and the leaves are dying, focussing on that part of the tree won't help you resolve the underlying issue. Tackling the symptom of a problem is simply triage. You need to find the root causes.

If you have a headache, you take a painkiller and it goes away. If the headache comes back, you take another. But if the painkiller doesn't work, or the headache keeps coming back, you go to see a doctor. You'll likely be prescribed a stronger painkiller, but this could mask a more serious underlying problem.

As a busy business owner it's tempting to take the quick fix option to your problems too. Sometimes this works, but in other situations, where the problem is systemic or chronic, it has little affect on the real problem.

Shit happens sometimes, don't worry about it. But if the same shit keeps happening in the same way, you need to get to the root of the problem to solve it. The positive effects of this action will filter through your business and inevitably take care of the result and success.

Amazing things happen when you're in the right environment surrounded by the right people.

And terrible things can happen when you're in the wrong environment surrounded by the wrong people.

Your environment matters. You want a positive environment that encourages focus, discipline and hard work. It should stimulate creativity and inspire you, making you feel good about yourself and what you're doing, and it should be aspirational. For some, this will be a quiet space, for others it will bustling. Your perfect view may be lakes and trees, or it's a metropolis skyline. Every year I take at least two working retreats, or 'work-ations' as one of my Mastermind members calls them. In fact, I'm currently writing this sat in a little cafe-bar overlooking a small private beach in Crete. This is the perfect working environment for me and this project. Find what works for you.

The people around you matter too. They can make the journey to success quicker and easier, or much slower and more painful. The right people support you, cheer you and hold you accountable. They believe in you but also challenge you.

Within my Success Groups and Extreme Growth Masterminds, I pride myself on having created amazing environments and cultures that stimulate, motivate, inspire and hold you accountable. While the education is awesome, I'll be the first to admit my success is as much to do with the environment I've created and the people I've attracted.

Be the steel core of your business.

Rethink the structure of your business. I favour what I call the 'steel core' over the traditional 'pyramid' model. When I think of the typical business structure, with the CEO at the top, I'm mindful of that great image of birds sat on telegraph poles. The CEO at the top shitting on the birds below, who shit on those below them, and so on and so forth. The poor sods on the bottom are literally covered in the stuff. This standard model takes responsibility away from the heads and puts it on the shoulders of the workforce. The steel core model sees the CEO or owner at the centre of the business, taking full responsibility for it.

As the owner, your business wraps around you. Your job is to support the business from within it; to deliver the strategy, vision, mission and values, and to manage the next layer out. That layer then manages the next layer out and so on. It's like ripples moving outwards from the owner in the centre, influencing and inspiring everyone within the company. Even if you've a very small business, it still works to see yourself as the centre of your business, rather than at the top of it.

Exceptional steel core examples include Steve Jobs, Richard Branson and Elon Musk. They each exemplify what their business stands for and sit firmly at its centre, not shitting down from the top.

ON MONEY

When business owners tell me money isn't important, I'm like, "What the fuck?"

The world is run on money. We can sit on the outside moaning about how others are using or abusing it, or we can get in the game. Money is fuel. Put it to good use and it will do good, use it negatively and it will do bad. But to deny the importance of money in business and, let's face it, in life, is delusional. Good people have wrongly been taught that to chase and make money makes them bad.

There's nothing that wouldn't benefit from you having more money. You may get a nicer house, a better car and greater opportunities in life, but you'll also be able to help more people and have a greater positive impact on those around you. The people who say that money can't buy happiness conveniently ignore the struggle, hardship and unhappiness that not having it can bring. At the very least, become wealthy to remove the discomfort and limitations that come with being poor!

Money is like electricity, making things light up. This is why I often refer to currency as 'curren(t)cy' – clever huh? Too many people sit on the outside of the flow of money, trying to grab a few notes or coins as it passes them by. Consider your own mindset towards money. Does it make you uncomfortable, excited, anxious? It's possible to change this, and to mentally and physically put yourself in the circuit.

Lead with commerce
and let your cause follow

Too many businesses are 'cause' led. What I mean by this is that they're run solely or predominantly for the causes they support, rather than for commercial factors and success. These business owners focus too much on helping people but not enough on the finances.

Don't get me wrong, businesses should definitely serve a purpose and contribute positively to society and the wider world. But I see too many well-meaning, well-intentioned and dare I say 'nice' small business owners struggling to make a go of things, simply because they're not taking care of commercial matters.

By its nature, cause is soft and fluffy while commerce is hard and gritty. Therefore, use commerce to punch into the marketplace and follow up with your cause. Get the money right and then deliver the positive impact you seek to contribute.

Your business is the best mechanism for successfully delivering your cause to the world. It enables you to reach more people and do more good. But to ignore or underplay the commercial aspects of your business limits the power it has to deliver your cause.

Think of commerce as the sharp, hard tip of an arrow that penetrates the world around you, enabling your cause and the good you do to follow through and make the difference you want.

Money first

Making money can be the product of your business or it can be the by-product of your business, but it must be the focus of your business.

Many business owners put money low on their priority list. They start their business with the higher values of purpose and giving great service. There's nothing wrong with either of these values, in fact I urge you to take these on if you don't already possess them. I just want you to put money first. Not to the exclusion of everything else, just as the initial focus for your business. Getting the money right enables your business to deliver on your other values.

We were a struggling business failing to achieve more than £50K. I was working up to 80 hours a week, getting into debt and burning out. The first year I set the theme of putting 'money first', I transformed the business. I didn't change any of my other core values, if anything I doubled down on them. Putting money first simply meant that business decisions had to pass the financial sanity test. If they passed, I progressed them. If they didn't, no action was taken.

Today my business is more successful, and I help far more people than I ever did when I was putting money third, fourth or even last on my agenda. Try it for yourself, put money first for one year and I guarantee you'll see a positive difference.

Let's get real.

You're unlikely to become a billionaire. The odds are against you becoming a millionaire. But 6-figures and multiple 6-figures that's open to everyone.

I saw a post on social media from a well-known business guru saying, "In America, there are 63 billionaires under the age of 40, will you be one?" There were about 200 "Hell yeah!" responses.

We're increasingly living in an unsubstantiated "Hell yeah, you can be anything" world. And whilst I love a bit of whoop-whoop, in the real world most small businesses don't even break the £100K mark. So, let's get real for a moment.

It's rare to become a billionaire. Out of the 1542 billionaires worldwide, the United States has the majority of them with 563. That's only 1 in 577,000 people. In the United Kingdom, we have only 55 billionaires amongst us, giving a probability of just 1 in 1.2 million that you'll join their ranks. Your odds of making a million in your business are higher, but they're still not great. I'm less bothered with the inane hollow chants of "Hell yeah!" than I am with the huge numbers of small business owners struggling to get their businesses off the ground.

Dream of making billions by all means. But first make sure you're putting the energy and commitment into driving your business to hit 5-figures, then go for 6-figures, and once you've hit that goal, then you can make 7-figures your goal. The odds are against you becoming a billionaire. But 6-figures and multiple 6-figures, that's open to everyone.

Pricing your product or service based on hourly rates is a mug's game.

Too many service-based businesses charge on an hourly basis. They treat themselves like a contractor. If you're a service business, your services can be 'boxed up' and priced similarly to a physical product.

Stop charging by the hour and start pricing on the positive impact you have on your client. You should be charging based on the outcome, and your prices should reflect the benefit and gain that your services offer.

I spoke with a business owner who was struggling to make a go of his business. He was charging his industry's average hourly rate, but delivering the results in half the time. This meant he was earning half the industry average per client.

Had he been charging a job rate and not by the hour, he would have earned the same per client as the rest of his industry, and in half the time. In addition, I pointed out that people will pay more for the same high-quality job completed in less time.

I suggested that he could be twice as expensive per result compared to his competitors, because he was getting the same results in half the time. This would 4X his earnings per client and 2X his earnings per hour! Overnight, he'd become one of the most highly paid people in his industry, giving the same great service he was already providing.

Be smarter with your pricing. See yourself as a business and your service as a product, and price accordingly.

Setting your rate based on being more expensive than some, but cheaper than others, is the laziest pricing strategy I know.

Don't be lazy by setting your prices solely on the market, positioning your service or products somewhere around the middle, where they're cheaper than some and more expensive than others.

Pricing is a fundamental part of your business model and strategy. Get it right and you'll thrive. Get it wrong and you'll struggle or possibly perish. Simply going for the middle will see you scrapping it out with the majority of your competition. Life will be hard.

It's much better to deliberately position yourself in the marketplace in such a way that you set your price, rather than letting the market do it for you.

Most small business owners would do better by setting out their stall as an exclusive, high-priced boutique, selling high-end products with large margins, rather than cheap mass-produced products. For example, you'd have a better chance of being successful selling a small range of expensive handbags in an exclusive shop, than selling larger quantities of low-priced mass-produced bags.

"Turnover is vanity, profit is sanity."

Yet more small business bullshit!

You've probably heard it a million times; I don't agree. Turnover is the perfect measurement of business growth. If you're focused purely on profit, it would be possible to become more profitable by shrinking your business. You could cut back on staff and reduce your premises, innovation and growth strategies. You'd make more profit, but you'd restrict your growth. As a long-term plan, it sucks.

Huge corporations need to be run for profitability, and of course, your business needs to be profitable, but for the small business entrepreneur wanting to grow, a turnover target is exactly what they need.

Profit is the sanity check that ensures your ventures and endeavours make sense. As long as you have a solid business model that delivers reliable profit, and you have a keen eye on your financial measurements, you're in great shape to chase turnover. For small business growth, that's sanity not vanity.

Like any relationship, the one between you and your business must meet both your needs!

Both you and your business have needs. You need to feel proud of what you're doing. You need to have a sense of purpose, to feel you're contributing to something and being of service. You have many needs; your business only has one. It's not burdened by the need to feel satisfied, loved or any other emotion. To survive and thrive it has one need; to make money.

Too many business owners suffocate or burden their business with their own values. Your business is its own entity, it has its own needs and its own rights; the right to survive and the right to thrive. Money may not be the most important thing in your life, but it's the only thing that matters to your business. Money is the fuel that feeds your business and enables it to grow. That said, it's good to place your values around your business and to build it as a force for good. But to ignore its only need, the need to be financially strong and successful, is negligent.

Understanding that you and your business each have needs, and that it's important for those needs to be met, puts the onus on you to make sure that your business delivers on your needs while you take care of its needs.

In fact, take care of your business's single need and it will take care of all of yours.

You can't get fairer than that.

ON SALES

Sell to £100K
Market to £1M

If you're not yet making a success of your business, stop marketing and start selling. Controversial, I know. If the idea of not marketing scares you, at least consider changing the ratio in favour of sales. The fastest way to hit £100K is to get out and sell.

There's so much bad advice out there for small business owners. Sometimes it's just dog-shit advice. Other times, it's generic and doesn't fit your specific business needs. You do need to market your business, but for marketing to really work, it often takes more money and time than you have when you set out. You can't afford to pay talented people to do it for you, so you get unskilled people instead, or just do a crap job yourself. You go at it half-arsed and you get half-arsed results in return.

The marketing strategy we implemented when we hit £250K turnover required the input of full and part-time staff, at a cost of £50K. This was the same strategy I was told to implement when I was running a £50K business with just me and Tracey. No wonder we couldn't make it work! With hindsight, I now know that the advice I was given was worse than useless; it damaged the growth of the business.

Get out from behind the marketing desk, where you can so easily be buried in bullshit activity, and get yourself into the sales hot-seat. Once you're making some decent cash, you can start to rely on marketing activity to continue your growth.

Step up and be the sales person your business needs you to be.

Your business needs to be fed, and you're the one who needs to feed it. You feed it with sales and it gives you the life you want in return. It's a fair exchange.

Many business owners didn't realise that when they started their business, they also took on a sales job. Many of them have never done sales and wouldn't be seen dead in a sales office. So it's no surprise that many don't step up to do the task.

But if you don't fill the role, who will? No one knows your business better than you. No one cares about your business more than you. No one looks after your clients better than you. Good sales people are often cost prohibitive. Cheap ones usually don't work. So, guess what? It has to be you!

Something to consider; I've never worked with or encountered a self-made business that grew organically to a £1M plus turnover, that didn't have its owner's butt seated firmly in the sales chair. You can try to prove that finding wrong, or you can accept it as a call to action and step up. You've all to win and all to lose; it's up to you.

Stop hiding from sales!

Come on, I'm calling you out here. If you're like many business owners, you're hiding from sales behind 'pseudo-sales' activities.

Maybe you've convinced yourself that posting on Facebook and LinkedIn, or even running ads on those platforms, is sales. Maybe you go networking under the guise of sales, but you're really going to meet friends and grab a free coffee or breakfast. Maybe you've convinced yourself that direct sales won't work for your business/product/client base* [*delete as appropriate]. I've heard and seen it all before.

I get it though. For many people sales can be intimidating, scary and even dent their self-esteem. But it must be done. Your business and your success demand it. Be brave and put yourself on the front line of your business.

I set a 28-day sales challenge in Success Groups, to break the bad habits and negative connotations some people have around selling. I created a real team spirit that made the challenge easier to complete. People soon desensitised, and many came out the other side surprised that they really enjoyed it.

If you can learn to love sales, you will be successful. I promise.

Sell more and sell for more.

The two key ways you're going to make more money fast:

    Sell more of what you do.
    Sell what you do for more.

You'll probably want to run both strategies at the same time.

If you've got capacity to handle more orders, you need to be selling more. If you're maxed out with orders, grow your operation so you can sell more. If your systems and processes are maxing out, you need to improve them so you can sell more. Basically, if you want to grow your business, you need to sell more. However, you also want to sell for more. If you sold 2X the products for 2X the price, you've just 4Xed your business. It's entirely possible to achieve this in a single year.

Don't make the mistake of thinking you can't charge more for what you do. If you think you can't, you won't look at how you could and it's important that you do. You may need a change of positioning, a change of proposition, or possibly a rethink of your target market. Rarely does the product or service itself need a massive overhaul to achieve these gains.

I've coached many business owners through doubling their prices and doubling again. In my own business, my 1:1 private coaching price has gone up over 18X in the past 8 years, nearly always in 2X increments. You can do it too.

Cut the crappy low-return tasks and double down on your sales activity.

Find the time to increase your sales activity. If you think you don't have time, you're wrong. There's time everywhere when you start looking for it. The sales activity you do is the most financially rewarding task in your business. Don't believe me? Take your turnover and divide it by the number of hours you genuinely spend on sales. I see many business owners achieve a decent revenue by spending just a few hours a week working on sales.

List all the tasks you perform, both within your business and your life, paying special attention to those that either yield little return or are low skilled. Start outsourcing the low-cost, low-skilled tasks, and double down on the sales activities that are already working for you. Personal tasks you could outsource include things like cleaning your house, doing the ironing, mowing your lawn or washing your car. Getting other people to do these tasks gives you back time to direct into sales activities.

You wouldn't believe how many business owners feel guilty about the idea of not doing their own household chores. They're equally relieved when I finally give them permission to stop that shit.

You're a high-flying entrepreneurial business mogul (or at least you will be), what the fuck are you playing at? Stop wasting time on the crappy low-return jobs and double down on sales!

Will it sell more cars?

Sales need to be at the forefront of your business. If you want big growth, you're going to have to sell more. Here's a great example of what's possible when a business focusses on sales.

A car dealership was failing and getting close to shutting its doors. A new business head was brought in to resolve problems and turn the business around. He moved into his office and immediately fixed a note to the outside of his door. Its simple message read,

"Will it sell more cars?"

No one was allowed to knock on his door with any issue or problem that, if solved, wouldn't ultimately lead to selling more cars. It soon became the dealership's mantra and core mission; if it doesn't sell more cars, it doesn't happen.

This simple but powerful extreme focus meant that every employee, from top to bottom, was solely focussed on selling more cars. Within the year, the dealership's fortunes turned around and it was back on the road to success.

If you need a similar outcome, have a similar focus and even try writing out your own note and fix it where everyone who needs to see it can see it. Having an extreme focus on selling more will lead to significant business growth.

ON SETTING AND STICKING TO YOUR OWN AGENDA

Goal setting is
the number one thing
successful people do.

To start setting your own agenda, and to find out more about my Kick-Arse Goal Setting programme, visit www.BiggerBrighterBolder.co.uk/KAGoals

Goals. Widely known to be the key ingredient in any quest for success. Yet hardly anyone sets goals. Of those who do, few do it properly and even fewer do it consistently. It's not surprising that hardly anyone achieves their goals.

Most of us were never taught how to set goals properly. And sadly, when we do get a book on goal setting or attend a course, it's often taught in an extreme way. One end of the spectrum being a, "Yeeha! You can do anything! Take your life and times it by a MILLION!" approach with no genuine structure, strategy or formula. The other end being a, "Yawwwnnn! Set practical, realistic, SMART goals".

Both approaches rarely deliver and usually leave people feeling disappointed, frustrated and reluctant to set goals again. There's very little practical AND inspiring goal setting resource material out there. That's why I created my own, with a full audio programme on how to set inspiring goals, an online system to track your progress, and an infrastructure to hold you accountable.

And, it works! In 2017, BBB Success Group members achieved more than 20,000 goals – an incredible average of over 266 short, medium and long-term goals each.

Get goal setting – done properly, it really delivers!

If you don't know where you're going, how can you possibly get there?

Do you have an agenda, and do you set goals against that agenda?

If you're like most people, the chances are you don't. In which case, you don't know where the heck you're going, which means you're probably on a fast-track to one of three places: you're either on autopilot playing out a self-fulfilling prophecy based on your upbringing, learnings and chance-happenings; or you're on someone else's agenda; or a combination of both.

If you're not working on your own agenda, the chances are you're working on someone else's. You're either working on your goals, or you're working towards someone else's. It's time to work to your agenda.

Take the time to think about what matters to you, what's important to you. Think about where you want to be next month, next year and in ten years from now. What do you want to create? What do you want to learn? What do you want to change or make better? What do you want your life to count for?

Think about your values, your passions and your purpose. Think about what makes you angry and what makes you happy, what stirs you and what bores you. By knowing where you want to get to, you'll be on the path to identifying your agenda and breaking it down into your own achievable goals.

If you don't have time to plan,
YOU HAVE TO PLAN!

Once you have a set of goals to work towards, you need a plan and a strategy for achieving them. If you don't have a plan, you don't really have goals. What you have is a combination of hopes, dreams and wishes. It's great to have dreams, but to make your dreams reality you need goals, plans and strategies.

Planning takes time and busy entrepreneurs often tell me they're too busy to plan. If this is you, you need to plan even more than the next person! The less you have of something, the more you need to plan how you'll use it. If you don't have a lot of time, you need to spend more time planning how you'll use the time you do have. It's completely counterintuitive and frustrates the brain – when you're busy, your brain gets stressed, and when it's stressed, it just wants to get going and do more, faster, harder... NOW!

If you have an abundance of money, who gives a shit? Do with it what you will. But if you have a lack of money, guess what? You need to take the time to plan how to use your money. If you only have so much energy, planning helps you make best use of it. In fact, planning helps you make the best use of any resource, by making you focussed, efficient and effective.

Goal setting is much more about what you won't do than what you will do.

If you're a busy entrepreneur, you probably have way more to do than you can ever realistically achieve. This is where goal setting is worth its weight in gold.

What you're unlikely to have been told is that goal setting is much more about what you're not going to do or achieve, than what you are. There's always way more you could do than you can do.

Good goal setting practices enable you to work out what isn't going to happen for now and what's being dumped altogether.

Setting goals is a process of subtraction and elimination as much as selection. Every member of BBB Success Groups and Extreme Growth Masterminds follows my Kick-Arse Goal Setting Programme, which is included in their membership. In the programme, we start by listing your most desirable, exciting, inspirational and aspirational goals. The programme then uses my proven process of elimination to leave you with a handful of absolutely Kick-Arse Goals that will deliver what you want and need for your business and life.

Goal setting needs to become a habitual way of life, as it's your consistency in setting and achieving goals that brings the greatest rewards. If goal setting is making you stressed, frustrated or miserable, you're simply not doing it properly.

You need a cast iron NO before you can have a strong YES.

If you say yes to everything, you're not actually saying yes to anything. To have a strong and absolute yes, you must first be able to say no. If you can't say no, you're not really saying yes, you're just not saying no. It's only when you possess the power to say an absolute NO to something that you're empowered to give a definitive YES.

If you're a people pleaser, this is a fucking nightmare because saying no to someone can leave you worrying you'll be judged, disliked or rejected. It's true, saying yes to every request often does make people like you, so saying no for a people pleaser is painful. Everyone needs a solid NO in their arsenal, but if you're a people pleaser like me, I'm talking directly to you right now!

Saying yes when you don't really mean yes actually leads to resentment and the feeling that you're being put upon. Saying yes when you haven't got the time or will to follow through inevitably leads to you letting others down. People pleasers, listen up, you're not pleasing anyone - not others, and certainly not yourself.

Saying yes to things not on your agenda pulls you away and onto someone else's agenda. You must have a strong no in you, so that when you say yes, you really mean yes. Play your own game, race your own race, fight your own fight and stick to your own agenda.

It's your commitment that shapes your life not your choices.

You'll often hear motivational speeches about how your choices shape your life, and how a single choice can change your destiny. While all deliberate acts start with a decision, it's not the decision that changes anything, it's your commitment to follow through with that decision that has the power to change your life.

Choices are fleeting and temporary in nature. They're easy to make and even easier to break. Choices are temporary, commitment is long term. One of my favourite quotes on commitment states:

"Commitment means staying loyal to what you said you were going to do, long after the mood you said it in has left you."

Yep, sums it up nicely. We all say yes to things, or make a decision in the moment that we regret and back out of later. Commitment is different. A commitment is a promise; a promise to yourself, to whoever else is involved, and to the outcome itself. True commitment is rare and incredibly powerful.

I was a self-confessed commitment-phobe. Making a commitment always felt like a trap, but it's actually a freedom. A freedom to stop double-guessing yourself or looking for the next best thing. A freedom to actually achieve shit and not just think or dream about it.

Are you fucking about?

Be honest with yourself. How often do you engage in activities and tasks that would score high on the fucking-about-ometer? It's a lot, right? It's amazing how many entries are on the 'fucking about' list, compared to the activities on the 'actually getting shit done' list. We can waste hours, days and weeks, and some have mastered fucking their entire life away.

I'll admit it, in many people's eyes my life might be considered boring. I chill out and have fun with my kids, I even have the occasional date night, but the rest of the time I'm either thinking about work stuff or I'm getting shit done. Now my health's back, having been ill for many years, I don't intend to waste a second.

A great check-in is to ask yourself every hour, "Am I fucking about?" It's your call what you ultimately decide is fucking about, but here are some guidelines to consider:

Anything that doesn't serve or isn't in direct alignment with your core goals or agenda.

Anything that is being used consciously or unconsciously to distract from something you should be doing.

Any meaningless activity that you accidentally ended up getting distracted with.

Accountability
gets shit done!

If you want to check out BBB Success Groups, go to:
www.BiggerBrighterBolder.co.uk

Accountability is the closest thing you'll find to a magic bullet for achievement and success.

The American Society of Training & Development did a study on goal achievement, and found that the chances of achieving a goal are:

10% if the goal is held only in your head
25% if you make a decision you will achieve this goal
40% if you attach a deadline to achieving the goal
50% if you create a plan to achieve it
65% if you commit to a third person that you'll achieve the goal
95% if you have specific accountability, such as an accountability group

Even if you have a goal and you've decided to go for it, a deadline and a well thought out plan, you still only have a 50% chance of achieving it.

You increase your odds to a whopping 95% chance of success just by committing to it and being held accountable for achieving it. Accountability is the largest single contributing factor to you achieving a goal, giving you an extra 30% chance of success.

The obvious conclusion for you is that you must set goals and have plans, but that you must also have genuine accountability built into the goal setting and achievement process. Goal setting with accountability is the backbone of BBB Success Groups and Extreme Growth Masterminds.

ON FEAR AND DOUBT

What is known is safe.
What is unknown is unsafe.

There's an evolutionary presupposition instilled in each of us. It's the assumption that what is known to us is safe and anything that is unknown, or that takes us away from that status quo, is unsafe.

This is why it can be hard to create real, genuine and substantial change in life. As soon as you start to deviate from your learnt rules for living life, the unconscious brain can apply the brakes. This internal resistance to change holds many entrepreneurs back from realising their full potential.

The unconscious brain manipulates us into acting in a way that's perceived as safe, based on learnt outcomes. For millions of years this worked well. If you were one of the lucky few to survive and reproduce, nature didn't want you screwing with the cycle, so it put your life in a pattern of rinse and repeat.

It can be hard to take action that creates significant change, even when all evidence shows that it's the right course to take. For example, to leave the job you hate, end a relationship that's miserable or even abusive, or to get your health in order, can all take huge amounts of effort, despite them being obviously the right course of action. Most change, even obviously positive change, can be perceived as unsafe by the unconscious brain. The problem is, evolution has set the bar very low for what your unconscious brain is willing to accept. You need to consciously and consistently work on raising it.

We thrive as a species by surviving as individuals.

Forget all that positive, "You're built for happiness and love and, and, and..." bullshit. You're built to survive, end of. Our species has been sculpted by millions of years of evolution, and for the most part, we couldn't walk two feet from our hole in the ground, tree or cave without being killed and eaten. Life was spectacularly hard and unsafe.

Therefore, while it's true that we have the emotional capacity to be happy, caring, loving, at peace... we're predominantly, as is self-evident, hardwired for fear, doubts and paranoia. It's how we survived as a species.

The brutal truth is that evolution and nature couldn't give a shit about your success, happiness or positive experience of life. These might be nice to have, but they're definitely not essential, not by a long shot. Survival, on the other hand, is a deal-breaker. We're not meant to thrive, we're meant to survive, and those are two very different experiences of life. We're built to survive so that our species can thrive, and with 7.5 billion of us on the planet, it's all going to plan.

There's so much more we could get from life, and yes, we really can be happy, fulfilled, fluffy bunnies, but we may really have to work at it.

Empowerment is not the absence of fear. It's the acknowledgement of the presence of choice in the face of fear.

As I've already stated, we only have a small degree of conscious influence over our lives. Fear is one area where we need to use that influence. Whenever we're faced with a situation that makes us fearful or doubtful, remembering that we have a say, even with the overwhelming presence of fear, can make the difference between our unconscious brain effectively running for the hills or hanging around long enough to hear us out.

We have a degree of influence as to whether we allow that fear to stop us or not. You need to learn to negotiate with yourself and be able to 'sell' your unconscious brain on taking the action that's right for you. Fear has the intelligence of a two-year-old, so you can't tell it it's wrong or being stupid. Just like a two-year-old child, the best approach is to demonstrate that something is safe.

Negotiating with yourself might be time-consuming and tiresome, but it's far less exhausting than constantly trying to push past fear using willpower alone, creating uncomfortable inner power struggles that you mostly lose.

Your fear is presenting itself as a barrier to something that the unconscious brain has learned or perceives as unsafe. As an empowered individual, you have a say in this. The more you build a relationship with your unconscious brain, the more it will learn to trust and listen to you.

Cross the threshold. That first step from the known into the unknown creates possibility.

Often, you just need to take that first step or make that initial leap to get you going. Doubt and fear are there to hold you back from whatever is perceived as a risk. But as soon as you take that first step, from what is known to you towards what is unknown, you're moving into possibility.

Instead of fear, try to think of the feeling as excitement. Excitement that things are about to change. Excitement that you're becoming someone who dares to take that step when it would be easier not to. The excitement of being on your own journey, deciding to live and not just exist, daring to thrive rather than merely survive.

Sometimes there's a need to take massive action and be all dramatic and statement-y about shit. But more often than not, you just have to take the next small step, then the next, and so on.

The succession of small steps soon mounts up and you start to increasingly put distance between where you were and where you want to be. This is how you walk 1,000 miles, one step at a time. As long as you keep moving forward, you'll continue to get closer to where you want to be.

Stop calling it the

BIG GAME

A football coach asked me why his players would play well all season, but crumble under the pressure of 'the big game', and what could he do about it? My answer couldn't have been simpler or clearer:

"Stop calling it the BIG GAME!"

This is something we see throughout sport. The racing driver who puts his car into the wall during the 'biggest race of his life'. The inspired, confident tennis player whose game turns to jelly during the final. The basketball player who misses the easy league-winning shot, and the footballer who spikes the ball up into the rafters in the penalty shootout for the cup.

It shows itself outside sports too. It's becoming a gibbering fool when asking out that hot girl or boy, or delivering that career-defining important presentation. It affects all people across all areas of life. The greater the stakes, the greater the risk and the more nervous and tense we become. The more fear and anxiety we have, the less we can think clearly, make sound judgements or control our bodily functions. We double-guess ourselves, we flounder and we turn to mush.

When you're competing in your own 'big games' in business; the big deal, the big pitch or the big audience, STOP CALLING IT THE BIG GAME! Think, it's just another presentation, pitch, serve or shot, just like all the ones before it. Keep perspective and you'll perform at your best.

Doubt, the harbinger of procrastination.

While our fears scream and jump around inside us, doubt sits almost silently at the back, quietly pulling the strings that hold us back. Doubt is meant to slow us down, to give us time to process information. Doubt isn't so much about something being unsafe, but more about something possibly being unsafe. There's no immediate threat, but it might not be safe, so tread carefully and take your time. The more doubt there is, the slower you'll go until you eventually stop altogether.

The antidote to doubt is certainty. With certainty we can be sure of when to take action, and what action to take. The more certainty we have, the more we commit ourselves to our endeavour. The more doubt we have, the less commitment we're willing to give.

If you knew for certain that your business would be successful and give all the rewards you could hope for, you'd probably work your arse off. But unfortunately, we can't be certain and that doubt messes with our game. We go half-arsed at things where we really should be going all in.

If we don't fully commit ourselves to our success, we won't be successful. But if we do commit fully to our success, we just might be successful. The possibility of success needs to be more powerful than the certainty of failure.

If we can't even prove that we or the universe actually exists, what the fuck are we so worried about?

I've included this thought to give a bit of perspective. Great thinkers, way smarter than me, have not only proposed but confidently stated that you, me, the universe, all of it, doesn't actually exist. And if it all does exist, it's not in the way we think it does.

Theories range from us existing in a multi-verse (rather than a universe), to a two-dimensional universe masquerading as a three-dimensional experience, to us all living in a computer-generated simulation. String theory itself has shown that computer code exists at the base of all creation.

There are theories from the ancient times to the present day which hypothesise that what we perceive as reality simply isn't reality. Quantum physics shows us that we exist in a universe where we, and most of it, are made from nothing. It's been postulated that we might all be brains in jars existing in a hologram. And none of these theories can be disproved. There's actually quite a significant amount of energy going into both proving and disproving that we actually exist.

The point is this; if we genuinely cannot be sure that anything is real, what the fuck are we so worried about?

I always end this sort of thinking by saying, "For the convenience of sanity, let's assume the universe is real." However, with so much doubt about that, it does beg the question, why take it all so bloody seriously?

ON MINDSET

Application

vs

Ability

As a busy entrepreneur wanting to grow your business, where do you put your time, money and energy? Sales training? Marketing? Lead generation? A new website? Facebook ads? SEO? Google AdWords...? The list goes on. It's a minefield!

You are already far better than the results you are getting! There's huge growth available to you, if you apply more of the ability you currently have.

The truth is, you already possess enough skill to dramatically improve your results. I'm talking 2X, 4X or more! What you do need to invest in is your mindset and attitude. Your mindset determines your attitude, and your attitude determines your actions and behaviour, which in turn dictate your results.

When was the last time you really knocked your own socks off with your performance? Was it last week? Last month? Perhaps several months ago? You need to understand that it wasn't a fluke, or down to the alignment of the stars. Those moments of exceptional performance when you were really 'on fire' were glimpses of your true capability. You've been getting insights into your awesomeness throughout your life.

Imagine having one of those moments every week. Imagine having multiple 'awesome moments' every single day. Then imagine consistently operating at this level. Where could you take your business?

Entrepreneurism is a mindset. Business is a skill set.

There are skills you can learn in business, whether it's cash flow, organisational skills, mergers, acquisitions, how to hire and fire, logistics or law. Learning and possessing these skills will certainly help you in business, but they won't set you apart. Oxford, Cambridge, Harvard and Princeton all churn out MBAs, and while I'm sure most recipients will get great jobs, that doesn't qualify them for entrepreneurship.

Entrepreneurism is an attitude. It's get-up-and-go. It's live or die by your own actions and activity. It's disruptive and non-conformist. Entrepreneurs solve problems and unsettle the status quo.

When I think about a great business person, I picture them sitting behind a desk pushing paper, oiling the wheels of industry, running systems and processes. If I'm honest, I picture a faceless suit running the businesses of an entrepreneur.

When I think of great entrepreneurs, I think of Steve Jobs, Richard Branson and even Gordon Ramsay. I see mavericks, inventors and creators. I see people who change the landscape of the world. I see people who stand out because of their 'E-Factor', their 'Entrepreneurial Factor'. Many hugely successful entrepreneurs aren't that great at business. It's not their business skills that set them apart, it's their MINDSET.

Success is a mind game.

It's well known that sporting performance is predominantly a mind game. A tennis player is unlikely to be wildly better or worse from one game to the next. Yet we regularly see athletes, players and teams being inconsistent in their performance. Their mindset is the biggest contributory factor to these inconsistencies.

I worked with a local rugby club that had barely won a game in the preceding years. They were heading for their fifth relegation in as many years. When I was approached to work with them, it was halfway through the season and they were at the bottom of the division. After their first mindset session, they won their next match. They absolutely trounced their opposition.

I continued to work with them for the rest of the season and things got better and better. If you took the second half of the season in isolation, they would have ended high in the league table. If you took the last quarter of the season in isolation, they would very likely have gone up a division.

It's impossible to be physically that much better that quickly. The only changes were mindset changes. It's been documented that winning is 80% mindset. Sir Clive Woodward, famed for taking the England rugby team to World Cup victory in 2003, was a huge proponent of having the right mindset and believed it to be at least 90% of success. His approach, philosophy and success certainly reflected this.

Where the mind goes, life will follow.

Your mindset and thinking lead the actions that direct the course of your business and life. What you focus on is where you're heading. In a previous career, teaching self-defence, I had a saying, "Where the head goes, the body follows." If you want to physically control a person, it would be pointless wrestling with them, or struggling with their flailing limbs. Take control of their head and you take control of their body.

It's the same in business and life. If your mind goes to negative places, your actions will follow and be reflected with negative results. If your mind keeps wandering to how you don't deserve something, or aren't good enough, your behaviour and results will be aligned with this. Money is a prime example. When people have a shortage of money, it's easy to obsess about the lack of money, focussing on shortfalls, debt, credit cards and unpaid bills.

Look at where the money is, not where it isn't.

It's tough, but focussing on a shortage of money will drive you straight in that direction. You won't solve your financial woes, or any other issue, by focussing on the end result of the problem. You need to obsessively focus on where the money is. The sales and up-sales opportunities, lead generation, networking, financial assistance or investment, unpaid debts and outstanding proposals. That's where the money you need is waiting for you.

You are living your life in a narrow bandwidth of possibility. Think bigger!

You're living your life within the narrow bandwidth of possibility that you have learnt, from the events in your life and the teachings that you've received.

It's common to get a grade C at school, and then be labelled a grade 'C' student. Both the school and you then expect you to continue to get C's. Low and behold, you get C's. The predictions are accurate because action follows expectation.

This is not an accurate reflection of how smart you are, but of how you approached your studies and exam. You approached the exam with a grade C expectation, studied like a grade 'C' student, revised like a grade 'C' student and ultimately performed like a grade 'C' student.

There have been many studies looking into students' expectations versus results, concluding that the expectations of the teachers, parents and student hugely contribute to the student's overall performance, which has no bearing on their actual potential.

Your expectations of you and your business determine how you take action, conduct yourself and resolve problems within your business. Higher expectations drive higher results. Changing your mindset to raise your expectations isn't easy though, especially when they've historically been set low. However, it's well worth putting the work in.

Acknowledgement of opportunity raises possibility and maximises your potential.

Okay, this might sound like a bit of a mouthful, but bear with me. Your potential is who you could be, and what you could achieve, if you were given the right opportunities and pushed yourself to your absolute limit. For example, had you trained like an athlete from an early age, you may not have ever won the gold medal for the 100-metre sprint, but you would have found your running potential.

Possibility is where the limitations sit. It's the conditioning from our parents, school and environment as we go through life. It's what sets our expectations of what we can 'realistically' achieve. If you'd never been exposed to the possibility that you could one day be a world-class entrepreneur, that possibility wouldn't exist for you and you wouldn't approach business as if you could.

Your experiences and learnings set your internal bar for what you consciously and unconsciously believe is possible. That limitation is one of the key things that holds you back from your potential.

To raise the bar for what's possible for you, you need to first see the opportunity. The opportunity that exists for you is far greater than what you've learnt or been taught. Acknowledging the opportunity that exists creates possibility. That possibility raises your game and gets you closer to realising your potential.

When you truly grasp this concept, it cracks your world wide open.

When you strive to achieve the impossible, you'll be called delusional. When you achieve it, you'll be called a visionary.

I was asked by a struggling client, "When should a person accept they're delusional?" Doubts were starting to creep into his thought patterns based on what the people around him were saying.

If you're ambitious, with a big vision and goals to match, it's easy for others to see you as delusional. It doesn't necessarily come from a bad place. It could genuinely be well-meaning, to protect you. But if you've a big vision and are determined to succeed, that shit doesn't serve anyone.

The history books are full of people who achieved what was believed to be impossible. These ambitious individuals were often labelled delusional, and even mocked for their efforts – right up until they succeeded, and were re-labelled a visionary.

Just because you're not succeeding yet, doesn't mean you won't succeed ever. Hopefully, you'll achieve your most ambitious goals and those around you will see your vision become a reality. But, even if you don't, it doesn't mean you were wrong to chase them. Some visionaries didn't get their 'visionary' status till long after their death, when they were eventually proven right.

As for the client who asked me the question, less than two years later he was heading up a multimillion-pound turnover business. How's that for delusional?

There's always more
left in the tank

The last time you went to the gym, did you stop when you thought you couldn't give any more, or when you physically couldn't give any more?

Discomfort and pain are impulses within the brain, triggered by messages from the body to stimulate action to keep the body safe. Take running on a treadmill. Impulses from the legs tell the brain they're under increasing stress and approaching the possibility of being harmed. That initial discomfort triggers a warning. You might not heed it, but you'll become conscious of it. As the activity continues, the discomfort intensifies and becomes pain, signalling a stronger warning to stop running.

But these warnings often trigger prematurely. Looking back in evolution, there was no sense in unnecessarily risking physical harm that could lead to death. Caveman never went for a jog, but there were times when he really did need to keep running, even though his legs hurt, to hunt or escape danger.

So, evolution created an override. When the task being performed is deemed non-essential, the brain more readily perceives pain. But with important and purposeful activity, the kind that leads to safety, the brain dials down the feeling of pain to keep you going.

Many of us allow discomfort to stop us long before we've run out of juice. Unless you're running right up to your physical limit, there's always a bit more in the tank.

ON FIGHTING HARDER

The most important trait of an entrepreneur is their fight.

One of the most important character traits in an entrepreneur is their fight. This isn't to say you should be tackling everything head-on, or battling your way through life.

I'm talking about grit, determination, resilience and taking responsibility for your life, instead of being a victim of circumstance. I'm talking about doing whatever it takes to achieve what's important to you. I'm talking about never compromising on your vision and standing strong on your agenda and goals. It's about stepping up when it would be easier to back down. It's about doing what you need to do, even when you don't want to do it. I'm talking about knowing what you want from life and tirelessly dedicating yourself to it. Taking chances and being brave. Jumping at opportunities to progress yourself or your business, even though it terrifies you, and then following through.

The fighter has conviction in spades and bucket-loads of commitment. They get up when they've been knocked down, and are stronger and more determined because of it. Fighting is about daring to live a life that matters, even when it's exhausting or uncomfortable.

That's the kind of fight worth cultivating because that's what it's going to take to succeed.

FIGHT HARDER!

When everyone else has gone home, the fighter asks two questions: What else can I do? What else will I do?

Those two questions separate the good from the great. They separate those in second and third place from those in the top spot. All successful people work hard. They put in long hours and aren't afraid of discomfort, sacrifice or going the extra mile.

What separates the fighter, the great, those in first place, is that when others go home they ask themselves these questions. They're as tired as those who've clocked off. They've done at least as much as anyone else. But before they follow everyone out the door, they ask these two simple, yet incredibly powerful questions.

The result could be one last sales call, or maybe three. It might be just one more set or rep in the gym. It might be just an extra 10 minutes or half an hour of taking action. It might not be much at all, but it's what separates the great from everyone else.

Jonny Wilkinson, the England rugby captain and one of the world's best rugby union players, would famously stay out on the pitch long after the rest of the team had gone in for showers. They all worked hard, they all gave a lot, but Jonny just gave that little bit more, and that's what separated him from the rest of the players. It put his name into the mind of the nation and set the benchmark for what it takes to be great.

Step up like you fucking mean it!

Our soft and safe lifestyles have made it okay to be half-arsed about our results. In the animal kingdom, nothing less than 100% will do.

Basic survival comes easily in our civilised world and, because of this, many of us have lost our fight. We're allowed to be passive and half-arsed in life. If we'd approached life like this in almost any other time, let alone way back in evolutionary timescales, we simply wouldn't have survived. The 'that'll do' mentality in today's society is robbing us of what we could have and who we could be.

We have unprecedented opportunity now because we're starting from a solid place of comfort. Roofs are over our heads. Food is in the fridge and, if it runs out, pizza is twenty minutes away at the end of a phone. Our cave-dwelling ancestors wouldn't be able to conceive just how easy we have it.

Yet we take it for granted and sit on our arses watching TV, on our PlayStation, or wasting our lives down the pub. Evolution pulls the plug on drive when we have enough, and most of us have way more than enough. We've lost our hunger, we've lost our fight!

Step up to life like you fucking mean it and embrace the opportunity ahead of you!

Step up when others back down and you'll separate yourself from the competition.

Here's a little mindset hack that will instantly see you pull away from your competition. First, understand that we're all human and we all have our fears, doubts and pain points. We might not all have the same ones, but we each have our own versions.

Now consider this: how often do you back away from things? How many times do you say no? How often do you fuck about, wasting time procrastinating? It's what your competition are doing too. It doesn't take much to get one step ahead.

The next time you're scared of something, or put off by the amount of effort or discomfort involved, just remember that most of your competition feels exactly the same. Every time you step up when you would normally back off, you're one step further from where you were, one step closer to where you're going, and one step ahead of your competition.

You can apply this simple attitude adjustment multiple times a day. Step up consistently and you'll leave your competition, and your old self, in the dust.

Fuck 'work-life balance!'

Give up on the 'work-life balance' bullshit. You'll never be successful trying to find a magic balancing point between working hard but not too hard. Look through the history books, read some autobiographies or just Google successful people, and you'll see that they all worked their arses off. There was no work-life balance. They knew what they wanted and they worked hard until they made it happen.

If you ever meet an Olympic gold medallist, ask them about their work-life balance. If you're ever fortunate enough to meet a super-successful business person, get tips from them about their magic work-life balancing act. Of course it's bullshit. If you want something, you have to work for it. The bigger it is, the harder you'll have to work and the more you'll need to sacrifice.

The idea of work-life balance appeals to the notion that we can somehow have the best of work and life, whereas in reality, you'll end up compromising both. Stop putting work and life on opposite sides of the equation and give everything you've got to everything you want.

If you're inspired by what you do, love doing it and have huge aspirational goals that excite you, fuck balance and go all in!

The four pillars of
entrepreneurial conditioning.

These pillars are inspired by my time in competitive kickboxing. If you want to take on the bigger fights, you need to condition yourself to handle the pressure and scale of those fights. If you end up in the ring with a champion and you haven't been conditioned to be there, it's going to hurt. A lot. Here are my four pillars of entrepreneurial conditioning:

1) Take the big hits. Business can be tough and the more successful you are, the bigger the hits you'll take. If you don't learn to roll with the punches and take a few good shots, you won't level up.

2) Make big, tough decisions. The more successful you become, the bigger and tougher decisions you'll need to make. If you don't condition yourself to make them early in your career, you'll never handle the pressure as your business grows.

3) Lose. Eventually we all lose, and the bigger the game you're playing, the bigger the loss could be. If you don't learn to regroup and recover from losing, you'll never handle the bigger losses you could face as you take your business to the next level.

4) Win. While it's important to condition yourself to take the big knocks and losses, it's equally important to win. Fortunately, you only need the occasional big win to keep you motivated.

Intent is not the same as intensity.

Don't let me scare you off with all this fighting talk. You don't have to be big, strong or a gobby arsehole to be a fighter. It's not about possessing a massive ego, being imposing or throwing your weight around. In fact, these are often the traits of weak people.

Being a fighter is about resilience, persistence and perseverance, not volume. A fighter comes in many shapes and sizes. Yes, there are the charismatic, larger than life fighters, but there are also the seemingly meek and understated fighters, people like Mother Teresa and Gandhi. The resilience of the fighter is what separates them from the pack. Their ability to bounce back from adversity, to lick their wounds in loss, and to keep moving forward with their vision.

There's a great saying, "It's not the size of the dog in the fight but the size of the fight in the dog." I love that!

Yes, Anthony Joshua personifies the fighter, but so does Mo Farah. Don't judge yourself as a fighter in terms of stature or ability to dominate. Measure in terms of heart, resilience and fortitude.

Don't mistake intensity for intent. Intent is a powerful force that can drive the smallest and weakest to the most heroic of action. Intensity can be externally impressive, but it doesn't pack the punch of rock-solid intent.

When the fight's long, it can sometimes be hard to see that you've already won!

I remember being battle weary. I was always looking for the next fight, the one that would end the need to keep fighting. But after every victory, I always found myself staring at the next battle. Then came a moment when I accepted that fighting was an inevitable part of the journey, and that it would only cease when I stopped progressing. Not progressing definitely wasn't an option. In that moment of realisation, I embraced my warrior within and continued to do what fighters do. I kept on fighting.

There are some rules that I've learnt along the way, two of which are:

Know when you've won. With all this fighting going on, it's sometimes possible to miss the fact that you've actually won. It's important to make time to take stock of your victory, to enjoy it before diving into the next battle. When you find your inner fight it can be addictive. Fighters fight, that's what they do, but they also enjoy their triumphs.

Know when you've lost. This can be very hard for the fighter to see, let alone acknowledge. It's in the nature of a fighter to fight to the death, after all, that's how you win. But sometimes, just occasionally, it's okay to let one go. Lick your wounds, reset, regroup and live to fight again.

ON PLAYING THE LONG GAME

Success is a long game.

Play the long game!

The older I get, the more time starts to compress. When I was twenty, a year seemed like a long time. When I was ten, it seemed like an eternity. Hell, at that age, the weekend never seemed to come. Christmases seemed eons apart, yet today I feel like I've barely put the decorations back in the loft before I'm getting them down again. Summer holidays come and go, as do birthdays, and this new experience of time brings new appreciations with it:

The future isn't as far away as you think.

Make it fucking count!

Instead of thinking in terms of days, weeks or months at a time, start thinking and seeing increasingly further into the future. There's truth in the statement that most people overestimate what they can achieve in a year, but hugely underestimate what they can achieve in a decade. Time is a friend and a powerful ally, if leveraged properly. The more we can plan ahead and take the appropriate steps today, the more likely we are to have the business and life we want.

The rules of success  **Consistently following them is the challenge.**

Bruce Lee said, "Long term consistency beats short term intensity." When you boil down the core components of what creates success, the rules are pretty simple. The rules aren't hidden or secret. They get spelled out time and again in autobiographies and success books.

The rules for success are:
    Have a powerful vision full of purpose and meaning
    Set goals
    Hold constant positive focus on the outcome
    Take consistent aligned action

At BBB I've gone a step further with these additional rules for long term consistency:
    Show up
    Keep showing up
    Bring your best
    Never give up

Consistency builds success. You need a way of holding yourself accountable for bringing your best to every single day. These simple sets of rules, while easy to understand, are hard to stick to. BBB Success Groups was set up predominantly to help people stick to these rules. They're not just important, they're vital to long term success.

If you want to check out BBB Success Groups, go to:
www.BiggerBrighterBolder.co.uk

Much of consistency is about managing your multiple and conflicting personality traits.

This may be a relief for you to know: there really are multiple personalities inside of you. You're not going mad, you're just like the rest of us. These personalities make themselves known through our thoughts and present themselves through our feelings. These conflicting traits create a battle within us, the outcome of which is reflected in the world around us and subsequently in our experience of life.

Long term success is a measurement of consistency. If you want to be consistent, you're going to need to take these voices and personalities in hand and get them into a more harmonious balance. This is critical if you're going to consistently bring your best to life and your goals.

If you lived every day as the best, most positive version of yourself, both you and your life would be pretty damn impressive. That's the gain available to you from rebalancing the traits within you. Much of the work we do at BBB Success Groups is about personal growth and I focus heavily on redressing this balance. To consistently be the best version of ourselves takes ongoing and consistent effort. But it works, and it's worth it.

It's not the ease of the road ahead but our strength to continue the journey that determines our success.

There's no easy path to creating a successful business. That doesn't stop millions of people buying into the promise of the 'magic pill'. But come on, we both know that doesn't exist, right?

The going can be hard sometimes, and the harder you're pushing yourself, your life and your business, the more it may push back. You'll have moments when things seem relatively easy, but they're often followed by times of graft, challenge and sometimes general shittiness. That's life, especially in business.

Your overall success isn't a reflection of the good times, it's representative of all those times you could have given up, backed off or simply gone back to bed, but you didn't. When you add all the times you leaned in, when you'd have been forgiven for throwing in the towel, that's where your success lies. Not in the big sales, the new hire or the successful marketing campaign, but the struggles, muddles and mind-bogglingly relentless arse-ache you endured.

When you see a successful person, don't see what worked for them as an indicator of their success, see what didn't work and how much fight, determination and perseverance they drew on to create that success.

As in life, sometimes business can be unfair. Persevere. Success favours the tenacious.

Life can be unfair. I struggled with the concept for a long time because, well, because it's not fair! I hate injustice. So I met the idea that life is sometimes unfair with resistance. If life is unfair, then nature, the world, even the universe is unfair. My resistance to this obvious truth initially challenged me, before it set me free. If life is sometimes unfair, then it's okay that sometimes shit happens. It's not nice, I'd prefer it not to be this way, but it's the natural order of things.

Then I saw that while life is sometimes unfair, it can be both positively and negatively unfair. I started to realise that sometimes I won when I didn't really deserve to.

My philosophy today is absolutely that life can be unfair in all possible ways, in my favour and against it. But, at the end of the day, month, year or life, everything will balance out. My life and my business will reflect an honest representation of what I put in. I might be unfairly treated by the world today, but it will work itself out in the final audit. It will for you too. So be tenacious and persevere, because that's what wins out in the end.

Success is a choice you make today for the future

Success takes time, even a lifetime. The choice you make to be successful is actually a choice you're making for your future. You won't see the rewards of your efforts for some time. You'll need to make sacrifices that won't pay you back for months or even years. What separates most people from their potential is their lack of ability to pay the price today for the rewards that come tomorrow.

One of the best choices you can make is to resist the small, immediate rewards of today for the greater, deferred rewards of tomorrow. Invest your time, money and energy today in those things that return the most later. Choose the temporary discomfort of creating change over the illusion of the comfort of the status quo. Your long-term success, whether it's financial, health, business or relationship, will be determined by your ability to invest in your future.

As a species, we've only been farming for ten thousand years. For millions of years before that, we were opportunistic and short-term focused hunter-gatherers. Our evolution is working against us, as is our disposable, consumerist society. Resist instant gratification and play a longer game – turn off the TV and pick up that business book. Put down the pizza and pick up the weights.

Every day that you don't do what you need to do to achieve your goals and create your future vision, is another day you don't get to enjoy it.

FEELING INSPIRED?

If you haven't done so already, download the accompanying workbook, and get started on addressing the gaps in your game. To download and watch the instructional video, visit:

www.BiggerBrighterBolder.co.uk/67Workbook

George would love to welcome you to his free Facebook community where he regularly shares ideas, content and Q&As:

www.facebook.com/groups/BiggerBrighterBolder

If you feel inspired to step up and accept the challenge of creating the business and success you've always desired, George would love to welcome you in BBB Success Groups.

If you're achieving more than £100,000 in turnover and want to double your business revenue in the next 12 months, you can apply to join BBB Extreme Growth Masterminds.

If you currently have a turnover exceeding £1 Million, George has the perfect Mastermind for you.

Find out more at: www.BiggerBrighterBolder.co.uk

or by emailing:
Tracey.Miller@BiggerBrighterBolder.co.uk

Bigger Brighter Bolder often hosts webinars and events. You can find out more details, dates and locations on the website, or by emailing Tracey Miller.

Follow George on social media, he'd love to hear from you:

Instagram.com/GeorgeSwift_MindsetMechanic
facebook.com/TheMindsetMechanic
Youtube.com/c/GeorgeSwiftTheMindsetMechanic
linkedin.com/in/GeorgeSwift
twitter.com/GeorgeSwiftBBB

BIG SHOUT OUT

I could fill a book with gratitude but, most notably, I would like to sincerely thank:

Tracey Miller, for her invaluable help with this book, and her tireless support for my many projects in their various stages of incompletion.

Michelle Power and Rachel Tapping, for their invaluable assistance in pulling this book together, copywriting, proofreading and sense-checking in turn.

Anne-Marie Lockett, for her kick-arse cover design and the creativity she brings to our entire business.

Chantal Bourgonje, for the typesetting, layout and internal design of this book.

My Mum, for always believing in the best of me and giving me the freedom to explore life without judgment.

My Dad, for indulging my incredibly heavy late-night chats as a child, and for giving me my first outlet to explore my ongoing questioning of life, the universe and everything.

Nick Jervis, for pushing hard against my resistance to changing the title of this book, and for eventually winning.

The amazing and inspirational members of BBB Success Groups and Extreme Growth Masterminds, for being open to receiving my guidance, and for joining and supporting me on my own entrepreneurial journey.

Michelle Power – www.powerofwords.media

Rachel Tapping – www.wordup-proofreading.co.uk

Anne-Marie Lockett – www.phase-two.co.uk

Chantal Bourgonje – www.cfordesign.co.uk

Nick Jervis – www.samsonconsulting.co.uk

ABOUT GEORGE SWIFT

George has been in personal performance for 25 years. In 2009, he founded Bigger Brighter Bolder (BBB). By focussing on the Mindset, Attitude, Performance and Cultural aspects of success, he has coached individuals, CEOs, senior executives, sales people and sports teams, to achieve significant performance improvements and business success.

In 2012, George launched BBB Success Groups for ambitious business owners. In 2014 he added BBB Extreme Growth Masterminds. In 2018 he launched BBB Success Groups online. At the time of writing, he was personally mentoring 90 businesses, including start-ups, 5-figure, 6-figure and multiple 7-figure businesses, supporting them as they achieve extreme growth.

George has an MA in Film, and has lectured in this subject, but his passion is entrepreneurism. Whilst his dramatic historical career changes have been described as 'fucking about', with hindsight this was his 'quest of discovery', seeking to discover how to make life work and why, for so many people, including himself, it often doesn't. Through his 1:1 private coaching, Success Groups, Extreme Growth Masterminds and this book, George invites you on the journey of success.